Sesame Street® Self-Care

Get Moving

Learn about Healthy Movement with Sesame Street

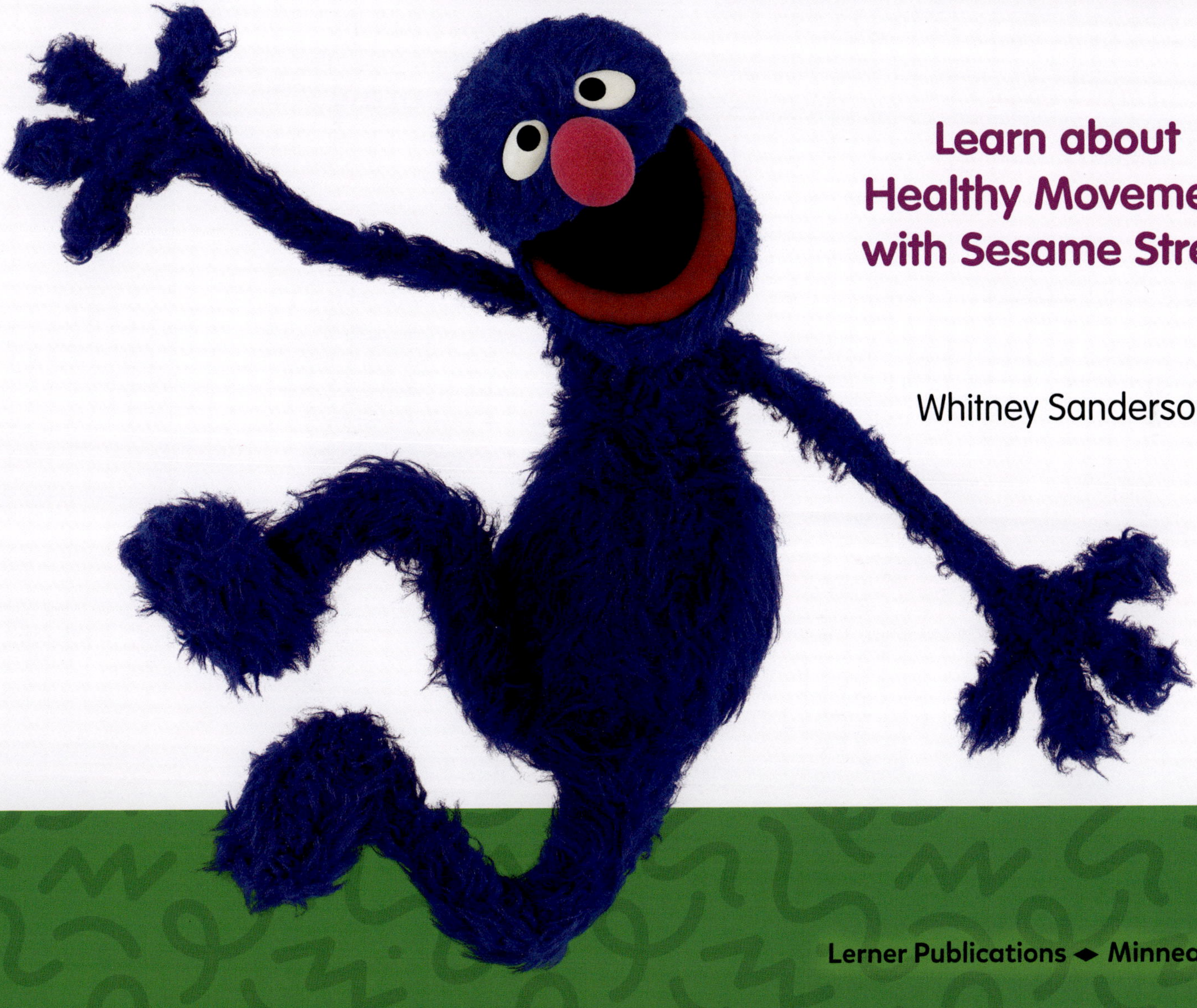

Whitney Sanderson

Lerner Publications ◆ Minneapolis

In this series, young readers will learn different ways they can take care of themselves! Come along as Elmo and his *Sesame Street* friends explore how healthy habits—like eating well and expressing your feelings—help you grow smarter, stronger, and kinder.

Sincerely,
the Editors at Sesame Workshop

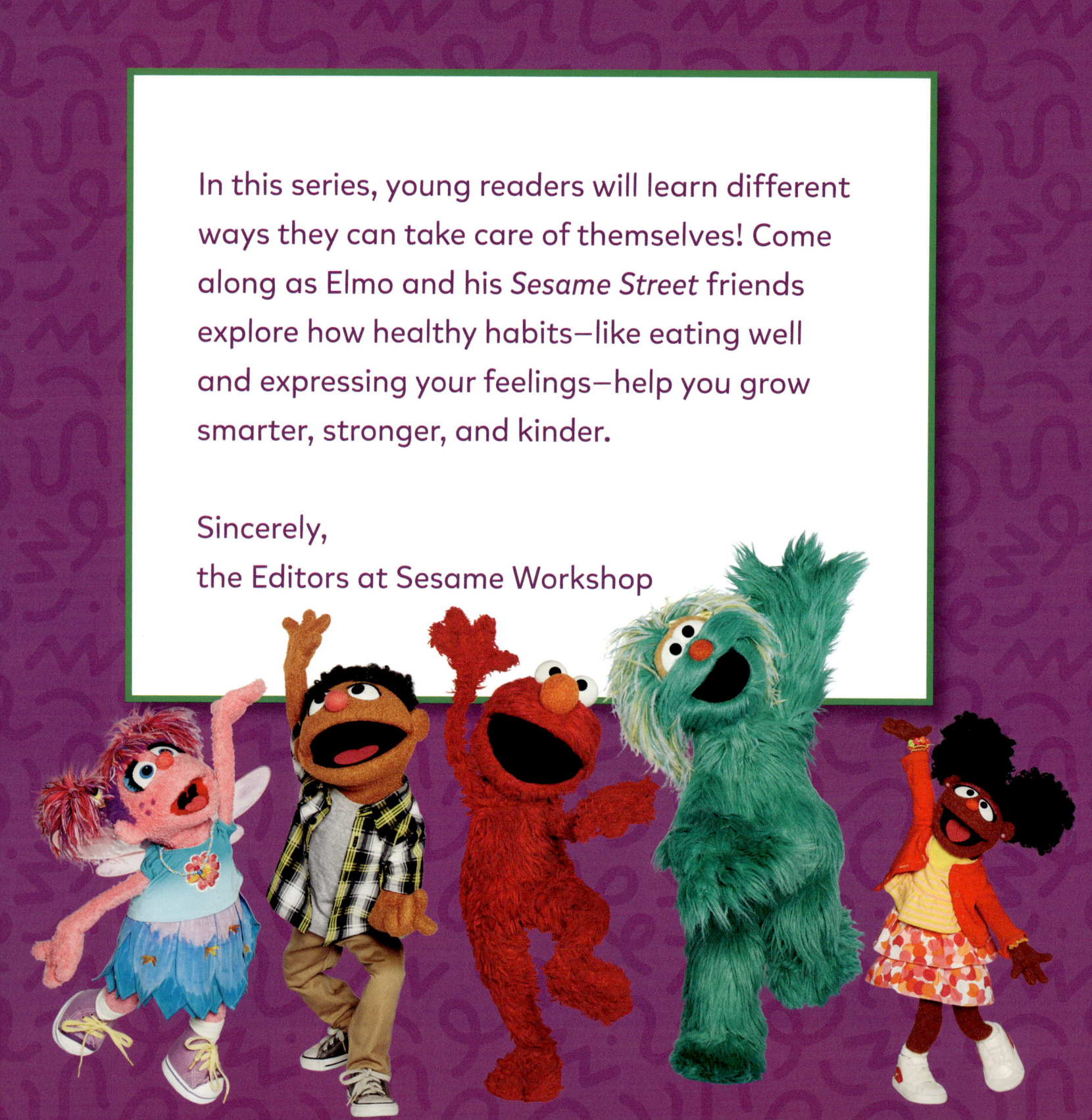

Table of Contents

Let's Get Moving! 4

On the Go 6

Healthy You! . . . 21
Glossary 22
Read More . . . 23
Index 24

Let's Get Moving!

Our bodies move in amazing ways. We can listen to our bodies and move in the ways that work best for us. It is important to move our bodies to keep us healthy and strong.

On the Go

Moving your body helps develop strong bones and muscles. It also helps your heart and your lungs.

Moving helps our minds too. It makes us feel good and helps us focus.

Riding my skateboard makes me feel happy!

Moving our bodies is a fun part of each day. You might stretch in the morning or play outside after school.

You can take a walk with your grown-up around the neighborhood or a park. You can swing, slide, and climb at the playground.

Elmo likes taking walks with Mommy, Daddy, and Tango.

Playing a sport is a fun way to move. You work together with your team and do your best. It's a great way to make friends!

You can move your body inside with freeze dance! Have your grown-up put on music and dance to it. Then when the music is stopped, you freeze. When the music starts again, dance!

Rainy days are fun with freeze dancing!

Some ways to move your body are calm and quiet. Yoga is one way. Yoga uses different poses to help you stretch and breathe.

Some poses are named after animals like cow, cat, and turtle poses!

This pose makes me feel calm and strong.

Moving every day keeps your mind and body healthy. You can find new ways to be active that work best for you.

I want to learn to roller-skate and play hockey!

Healthy You!

Have a dance party! Ask your grown-up to put on some music. Get up and dance to it! Try different moves. Maybe you dance to slow songs or fast songs. How does your body feel during each dance?

Glossary

focus: to pay attention to what you are doing

neighborhood: a group of people living close to one other

team: a group of people working or playing together

yoga: special movements or breathing that help your mind and body

Read More

Burk, Rachelle. *Stomp, Wiggle, Clap, and Tap.* Naperville, IL: Callisto, 2024.

Posner-Sanchez, Andrea. *1, 2, 3, Exercise with Me! Fun Exercises with Elmo.* New York: Random House Children's Books, 2022.

Sanderson, Whitney. *Be a Friend: Learn about Healthy Friendships with Sesame Street.* Minneapolis: Lerner Publications, 2025.

Photo Acknowledgments

FatCamera/Getty Images, pp. 4, 18; Images By Tang Ming Tung/Getty Images, p. 6; JulPo/Getty Images, p. 9; AscentXmedia/Getty Images, p. 10; Kinzie Riehm/Getty Images, p. 13; Thomas Barwick/Getty Images, p. 14; fizkes/Shutterstock, p. 17; CocoSan/Getty Images, p. 20. Design elements: Dedraw Studio/Shutterstock.

Index

minds, 8, 20
muscles, 6

sport, 14
walk, 5, 12

yoga, 18

To Faisal

Sesame Street® and associated characters, trademarks and design elements are owned and licensed by Sesame Workshop. © 2025 Sesame Workshop. All rights reserved.

International copyright secured. No part of this book may be reproduced, stored in a retrieval system, or transmitted in any form or by any means—electronic, mechanical, photocopying, recording, or otherwise—without the prior written permission of Lerner Publishing Group, Inc., except for the inclusion of brief quotations in an acknowledged review.

Lerner Publications Company
An imprint of Lerner Publishing Group, Inc.
241 First Avenue North
Minneapolis, MN 55401 USA

For reading levels and more information, look up this title at www.lernerbooks.com.

Main body text set in Mikado. Typeface provided by HVD.

Designer: Laura Otto Rinne
Lerner team: Martha Kranes

Library of Congress Cataloging-in-Publication Data

Names: Sanderson, Whitney, author.
Title: Get moving : learn about healthy movement with Sesame Street / Whitney Sanderson.
Description: Minneapolis : Lerner Publications, [2025] | Series: Sesame Street self-care | Includes bibliographical references and index. | Audience: Ages 4-8 | Audience: Grades K-1 | Summary: "Get up and get ready to move with your friends from Sesame Street! Young readers learn the importance of exercise, fun ways to move, an indoor activity for rainy days, and more"— Provided by publisher.
Identifiers: LCCN 2024008833 (print) | LCCN 2024008834 (ebook) | ISBN 9798765643709 (library binding) | ISBN 9798765662403 (paperback) | ISBN 9798765657997 (epub)
Subjects: LCSH: Exercise—Juvenile literature. | Health—Juvenile literature. | Sesame Street (Television program)—Juvenile literature.
Classification: LCC RA781 .S245 2025 (print) | LCC RA781 (ebook) | DDC 613.7/1—dc23/eng/20240524

LC record available at https://lccn.loc.gov/2024008833
LC ebook record available at https://lccn.loc.gov/2024008834

Manufactured in the United States of America
1-1010919-52411-7/23/2024